Bugs

Tarantulas

by Trudy Becker

FOCUS READERS
PIONEER

www.focusreaders.com

Focus Readers is distributed by North Star Editions:
sales@northstareditions.com | 888-417-0195

Produced for Focus Readers by Red Line Editorial.

Photographs ©: Shutterstock Images, cover, 1, 4, 6 (top), 6 (bottom), 8, 10 (top), 10 (bottom), 12, 14, 17, 18, 20

Library of Congress Cataloging-in-Publication Data
Names: Becker, Trudy, author.
Title: Tarantulas / Trudy Becker.
Description: Lake Elmo, MN : Focus Readers, [2023] | Series: Bugs | Includes index. | Audience: Grades 2-3
Identifiers: LCCN 2022035478 (print) | LCCN 2022035479 (ebook) | ISBN 9781637394526 (hardcover) | ISBN 9781637394892 (paperback) | ISBN 9781637395622 (pdf) | ISBN 9781637395264 (ebook)
Subjects: LCSH: Tarantulas--Juvenile literature.
Classification: LCC QL458.42.T5 B43 2023 (print) | LCC QL458.42.T5 (ebook) | DDC 595.4/4--dc23/eng/20220726
LC record available at https://lccn.loc.gov/2022035478
LC ebook record available at https://lccn.loc.gov/2022035479

Printed in the United States of America
Mankato, MN
012023

About the Author

Trudy Becker lives in Minneapolis, Minnesota. She likes exploring new places and loves anything involving books.

Table of Contents

Chapter 1

A Tasty Catch

A tarantula creeps along the forest floor. It is hunting a small lizard. The tarantula's hairy legs reach out. It grabs the lizard. The tarantula bites. It got its meal.

Tarantulas are some of the biggest spiders in the world. They live in warm places like rainforests and deserts. Most live in holes in the ground. At night, they come out to hunt their **prey**.

Fun Fact

More tarantulas live in South America than anywhere else.

Chapter 2

Legs and Jaws

Like all spiders, tarantulas have eight legs. Their legs help them move and grab prey. Tarantula bodies have two parts. The legs attach to the front part. The back part is the **abdomen**.

abdomen
leg
jaw
pedipalp

Tarantulas have strong jaws. The jaws have sharp fangs. They help tarantulas kill prey. Tarantulas also have **pedipalps**. These parts look like small legs. They help tarantulas sense things.

Fun Fact

Tarantula fangs can be 1 inch (2.5 cm) long.

Chapter 3

Mealtime

Tarantulas use **venom** when they bite. The venom makes their prey stop moving. Then it's easier for tarantulas to eat their meal.

Tarantulas don't swallow solid food. They drink their food. Tarantulas put a harmful material into their prey. It turns them into **liquid**. Then tarantulas suck up their meal.

Fun Fact

Some tarantulas drag food back to their holes before eating.

Harmful Hairs

Tarantulas are **predators**. But they can be prey, too. So, tarantulas have spiky hairs to fight off threats. They use their legs to kick off the hairs. The hairs sting predators' eyes and skin. Then the tarantulas can run away.

Chapter 4

Tarantula Life

Tarantulas are **carnivores**. They often eat insects like beetles. Some eat frogs or mice. Some even eat birds.

Tarantulas can spin silk. Sometimes they use their silk to help build nests. Females also use silk to wrap eggs. They keep the eggs safe until it is time to hatch.

Fun Fact

Tarantulas **molt** as they get bigger. They grow new parts and shed the old ones.

FOCUS ON

Tarantulas

Write your answers on a separate piece of paper.

1. Write a sentence that explains the main idea of Chapter 3.
2. What would you do if you saw a tarantula in the wild? Why?
3. What do tarantulas eat?
   - A. insects
   - B. eggs
   - C. plants
4. Why do tarantulas drink their food?
   - A. They think it tastes better as a liquid.
   - B. They don't have teeth for chewing.
   - C. They aren't strong enough to hold solid pieces.

Answer key on page 24.

Glossary

abdomen
The back part of a spider. It contains the heart.

carnivores
Animals that eat meat.

liquid
Not solid or gas.

molt
To lose an older covering so a new one can grow in its place.

pedipalps
Body parts attached to a spider's head. They are used for the sense of touch.

predators
Animals that hunt other animals for food.

prey
Animals that are eaten by other animals.

venom
Poison that comes from an animal's sting or bite.

To Learn More

BOOKS

Golkar, Golriz. *Tarantulas*. Minneapolis: Abdo Publishing, 2022.

Jaycox, Jaclyn. *Tarantulas*. North Mankato, MN: Capstone Press, 2020.

NOTE TO EDUCATORS

Visit **www.focusreaders.com** to find lesson plans, activities, links, and other resources related to this title.

Index

Answer Key: 1. Answers will vary; **2.** Answers will vary; **3.** A; **4.** B